Exploring

Church Development

Mike Booker

Director of Mission and Pastoral Studies,
Ridley Hall, Cambridge

GROVE BOOKS LIMITED
RIDLEY HALL RD CAMBRIDGE CB3 9HU

Contents

Acknowledgements

I would like to express my thanks to several church leaders who gave me important insights into the experience of working with Natural Church Development. Some of their stories are told below, but space has not permitted me to include all of them. My thanks are due also to those members of the Grove Evangelism Group and a number of other people who have contributed many important ideas in the course of my investigations.

The Cover Illustration is by Peter Ashton, adapted from NCD

Church Army and the Grove Evangelism Series

Church Army has over 350 evangelists working in five areas of focus, at the cutting edge of evangelism in the UK. It co-sponsors the publication of the Grove Evangelism Series as part of its aim of stimulating discussion about evangelism strategies, and sharing its experience of front-line evangelism.

Further details about Church Army are available from:
Church Army, Independents Road, Blackheath, London SE3 9LG.
Telephone: 020 8318 1226. Fax: 020 8318 5258.
Registered charity number: 226226

First Impression August 2001
ISSN 1367-0840
ISBN 1 85174 473 8

1
Introduction

This booklet is a personal look at a new approach to church life called Natural Church Development. This approach arises out of church growth studies and provides a new way of assisting churches in the task of mission. I am attempting to assess Natural Church Development (NCD) objectively, to enable the local church leader to evaluate how it can help evangelism at a congregational level.

Church growth theory, out of which NCD has grown, raises concerns in the minds of some observers. While many of the aims of the Church Growth Movement (in particular the overarching conviction that God intends his church to grow) may be laudable, I have shared the unease of many that somehow the packages and strategies proposed do not have a 'gospel feel' about them. With all the bright-eyed conviction of those who saw in DDT the eradication of malaria, church growth theories have promised the transformation of the life of the western church, yet have sometimes not only failed to deliver but also brought with them a range of questionable side-effects. Focus on numerical targets can leave ministers and congregations under pressure to achieve and disillusioned if the magic number is not attained. The Homogeneous Unit Principle in particular (most eloquently defended in C Peter Wagner's, *Our Kind of People*[1]), with its suggestion that churches grow most easily when they are gatherings of the same social, ethnic or national groupings, has long been criticized and seems even less easy to defend in the post-apartheid era.

In the UK context the one most clearly-identifiable programme for evangelism (and by implication at least, for church growth) to emerge during the Decade of Evangelism has been the Alpha course. While highly effective in a range of settings, the 'one size fits all' approach of Alpha can lead to its unconsidered adoption by busy clergy without very extensive consideration as to whether it is actually the best way forward for that church at that time. Mark Ireland in his thesis on process evangelism has identified desperation as one of the key reasons for adopting Alpha.[2]

Natural Church Development offers a way into some aspects of church growth thinking without simply going for numerical targets and homogeneous units. It provides an overview of church life which may point to one of a wide range of ways forward, quite possibly using Alpha, but not after a simple 'Alpha or nothing' choice which some may feel they face.

My interest in NCD stems from encounters with church leaders who had read the book and found something refreshing and inspiring in its approach, followed by the chance to follow up this interest through two meetings with Christian

---

1   C Peter Wagner, *Our Kind of People* (John Knox, 1979).
2   The thesis is available at http://www.evangelism.uk.net

Schwarz, the German church growth scholar who stands behind the programme. Visits to several churches which are working with the materials, some of which are directly reflected in this booklet, gave a fuller picture of how the process can work out in practice. What follows is not written out of a conviction that NCD is the answer to the needs of the church at the start of a new Millennium, nor even that it is the most important package around for the average church leader. What NCD does provide is one way of taking a step back, looking with fresh eyes at what the local church is up to, and beginning to get some pointers of what the future directions might be. It is most certainly not without its limitations and drawbacks, but I believe these need to be seen as just that, limitations to what is nevertheless a very significant tool in the hands of the thoughtful church leader.

2
What is Natural Church Development?

To most church leaders the idea of natural church development is something it is hard to disagree with. Along with being kind to children and animals and opposed to sin, looking for natural church development is something of an unassailable ideal. The problem facing most churches in our current society is that development does not seem to come very naturally. Left to themselves (in 'inherited mode,' to use one piece of current terminology) most churches do not really develop, they decline—or at least they do develop, but into older and generally smaller congregations as the years pass. Church growth programmes and strategies for the (easily alliterated but less easily achieved) transition from maintenance to mission may be available in a number of guises, but they may not feel particularly natural in the UK context. In particular, most church growth writing is closely related to American or Two-Thirds World contexts in which church life looks and feels very different, and the transfer to a British situation can be strained to say the least.

Natural Church Development is both the title of a book[3] and the name of an approach to church growth which it outlines. Developed by Christian Schwarz of the Institute for Church Development in northern Germany, NCD is the fruit of many years' research and development. Schwarz's beginnings are within the school of church growth thinking based at Fuller Theological Seminary in Pasadena, but he followed this earlier work with an extensive international survey which was instrumental in leading him towards a significantly revised approach to church growth. The survey covered 1000 churches in 32 countries, across a range of theo-

---

3   Christian Schwarz, *Natural Church Development, a Practical Guide to a New Approach* (BCGA, 1996).

logical, denominational and linguistic divides. The survey results and his own theological convictions led Schwarz to produce a new approach to church life based fundamentally upon church health rather than numerical growth. The basics of the approach are laid out in the main book, complemented by the *Natural Church Development Implementation Manual* (BCGA, 1998), and Schwarz's theological rationale for his thinking, *Paradigm Shift in the Church* (Church Smart, 1999).

Being at heart a German project which is still in the process of translation into English, a considerable stock of resources remains to be translated. Coming from the German, the terminology used by NCD can at times be unusual, but on the other hand it also sounds a bit different, not in the expected mould. Something new is going on! Other refreshingly different things emerge, for example the strongest link to a high level of church health occurs with positive responses to the statement: 'There is a lot of laughter in our church.'[4]

So what exactly are the distinctives of NCD? Some of the essential points are as follows:

- Principles rather than models
- Quality rather than quantity
- The significance of the minimum factor
- A biotic approach to church life. That is, a view of the church as a living organism rather than an organization.

Principles Rather than Models

How can the hard-pressed and sometimes dispirited congregation hope to see growth? In response to this question, the answer has often been to look at large, growing churches (or at least, at large churches which have grown in the past) and to attempt to emulate them. From the small-church choir struggling to cope with an anthem somebody heard at the cathedral to the eager evangelical congregation launching into Willow-Creek style seeker-services, the temptation is to think that something which works in one place will provide a formula which can be transplanted elsewhere with similar effects. Sadly, the experience of reality often leads to disappointment. At best the approach of the large church suffers from increased dilution as the scale or cultural setting of church life gets further from the original. At worst what results is the 'we tried that once but it doesn't work here' mentality which can stifle new ventures of any kind in the future.

NCD makes the bold claim to be able to identify those universally applicable principles which correlate strongly with healthy church life across the range of churches surveyed internationally. Although the principles themselves may be transferable, their implementation will vary from place to place, so that one healthy church may look very different from another. Genuine church health depends upon fittedness to the specific context, be that the denomination and theology of the church concerned or the local cultural setting.

4   Schwarz, *Natural Church Development*, p 37.

Quality Rather than Quantity

At heart, NCD is about health and the quality of church life, not about numbers. In the process of statistical analysis of the initial international survey data, Schwarz's institute detected eight key quality characteristics which consistently correlated with each other and with overall church health. If every quality characteristic exceeded the magic 65% level (that is, a level significantly above the national average of churches surveyed), then the church was found without exception to be numerically growing. However, numbers, or at least numerical goals, are not the primary concern of NCD. The focus is upon the quality of church life, with the accompanying confidence that God will provide numerical growth where the church is healthy.

The eight quality characteristics identified (in no particular order of priority) are as follows:

- Empowering leadership
- Gift-orientated lay ministry
- Passionate spirituality
- Functional structures
- Inspiring worship services
- Holistic small groups
- Need-orientated evangelism
- Loving relationships

What matters most in the eight quality characteristics is the adjective describing each one. Thus, most churches have leadership, but the key thing is that it should be empowering; most congregations see expressions of lay ministry but NCD is concerned that it should be gift-orientated; and so on. Although not linked to any denominational strand, NCD is explicitly within the Reformation tradition. It presupposes the rightness of the theology of the reformers and of the pietists (broadly equivalent to Evangelicalism in the English-speaking world). More specifically, in its contemporary application there is an assumption that certain things, for example an understanding of evangelism in terms of personal conversion, and the presence of small groups within the church, are not only desirable but already present in the participating congregation. While going for wide applicability, there are parameters beyond which the quality characteristics may not seem applicable.

Those familiar with church growth literature may detect a familiar feel about the list, but it does contain some important differences from the characteristics of growing churches more often found in books based on classical church growth theory. Some of these changes have emerged during the course of Schwarz's research, particularly empowering leadership, which began as 'the goal-orientated pastor.' The softer and more participative 'feel' of the revised terminology reflects a modification of previously-held assumptions in the light of extensive worldwide investigation.

Likewise, as mentioned above, there is no Homogeneous Unit Principle. This is replaced by Schwarz with only a recognition of the need for loving relationships. The challenge, as Christ instructed his disciples, is to love one another. That most certainly should be possible across a diversity of types and conditions of people, and our finding it easier among people like ourselves may be more an expression of human sin than of God's design. After all, as Jesus pointed out, even the tax-collectors got on well with people who got on well with them (Matt 5.43–47)!

While fitting most easily into a broadly evangelical church culture, the quality characteristics are nevertheless applied to a wider range of settings than a number of other authors seem to envisage. George Barna, for example in his *The Habits of Highly Effective Churches* (California: Regal Books, 1999) states that church growth seems to need at least twenty minutes of uninterrupted worship songs in any given service! Schwarz is open to considerably more variety than this, commenting in the *Implementation Manual*: 'This is the area where you find most diversity of style (and liturgical 'rules'), so it is impossible to give a single model which is useful for every church.'[5]

The results of the research into quality characteristics include some fascinating discoveries. Small churches, for example, tend on a world scale to grow faster and to have a higher quality of life than larger churches. Larger churches, it seems, can run more impressive programmes but may suffer from a lack of involvement on the part of many members of the congregation and so have lower quality scores. Seeker services seem to have very little impact on a world scale, whereas the use of outside consultants correlates strongly with church growth.

The Significance of the Minimum Factor

So how do we juggle all that lot? If there are eight quality factors to be kept up to scratch all the time, how can any church hope to keep working on them all? The key thing is the minimum factor. A church will be as healthy as its weakest characteristic, since this is the thing which will be primarily holding back the growth God desires. Schwarz uses a number of analogies from life and from natural processes to communicate this point. For example, if a diet is generally good but deficient in one vitamin, ill health will result because of that one weakness regardless of what is going on elsewhere in the pattern of nutrition. Similarly a field will be able to produce crop yields in proportion to whichever essential fertiliser is present in the smallest quantities.

The minimum factor hypothesis is revealed most helpfully by the milk-barrel image. For a number of church leaders, grasping the significance of this illustration has probably been the single most important learning experience in encountering NCD. In Switzerland, milk has traditionally been kept in barrels or churns made from vertical slats of wood. If these slats are of different lengths then the amount of milk which can be held will depend upon the height of the shortest

---

5   Schwarz, *Implementation Manual*, p 90.

slat. Increasing barrel capacity can be achieved only by making the shortest slat longer—any changes to other parts of the barrel are unproductive and a waste of energy. The barrel will only be able to hold more milk if the shortest slat is lengthened.

The minimum barrel

The shortest stave determines the amount of water the barrel can hold

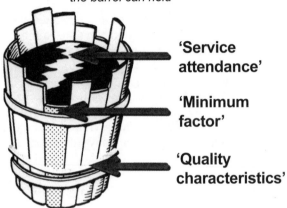

'Service attendance'

'Minimum factor'

'Quality characteristics'

So, to apply this image to church life, the cosy congregation which cares for its members well, the evangelistically-thrusting evangelical fellowship and the church which is known for the excellence of its worship (be it choral or charismatic) all very clearly have significant strengths. A case could be made for love, for evangelism or for worship to be the single most important characteristic of church life, and each church could choose to continue to focus on its own top priority. NCD insists that while each emphasis is of great importance, truly balanced and healthy church life, and by implication sustained growth, can only be achieved if the minimum factor is addressed. Thus a loving church which makes the effort to look outward, an evangelistic church which recognizes the need to care for both congregation and converts or a worshipping church which faces up to the untapped gifts of the passive recipients in the pews each Sunday will be healthier and more open to natural (rather than forced) church growth as a result.

In response to the relative weakness of the minimum factor, Schwarz then encourages the church to use its strengths to address the weaknesses. This could then lead to the transformation of the situations mentioned above. Love can flow out into concern for those beyond the congregation. Evangelistic energy which sees people's need of God can be redirected to focus on the need to keep close to God. Worship can be transformed to employ a wide range of gifts rather than remaining a slick performance by the minority. In each case the strengths of the church are exercised, and used to address the weakest part of church life.

Once the minimum factor has been addressed, further growth in church health can follow, and will continue until the next minimum factor makes its presence felt. This will then in turn need to be addressed if further growth is to be possible.

A Biotic Approach to Church Life

Once the minimum factor is identified, NCD encourages a 'biotic' approach in response. Inspired by Jesus' promise to Peter, 'I will build my church' (Matt 16.18) and by the parables of the kingdom, Schwarz identifies the 'All By Itself' principle. Growth is fundamental to God's design in creation. If we believe the church is also fundamental to God's purposes then we should should expect growth to be something which will occur naturally if only we let it do so.

Here some readers (to use biological terminology) may be wilting somewhat, and my conversations with church leaders have suggested that they will not be alone. In the *Natural Church Development* book a list of biotic principles draws on patterns in the natural world as illustrations of the ways in which a church should grow naturally. The key to what is going on should be a balance between the super-spiritual ('let go and let God') and the purely technical ('follow this formula and your church will grow by 10% in the next year'). Life needs both energy and structures, and Schwarz encourages a vision of church life where the way of thinking instinctively draws inspiration from the growth processes of the natural world. Most churches, he claims, tend towards one end or the other of the energy versus structures continuum, whereas NCD enables a balanced partnership between the two.

The dedicated reader will find this expounded at greater length in the later sections of the book (See pp 61–82) and also in more detail in *Paradigm Shift*. The church which simply adopts the NCD process will, in theory at least, be guided along paths which allow natural, 'biotic' church growth to develop.

3
Putting it into Practice

So how does it work out in practice? Schwarz's books outline the stages of implementing the approach as follows:

- build spiritual momentum
- determine your minimum factors
- set qualitative goals
- identify obstacles
- apply biotic principles
- exercise your strengths
- utilize biotic tools
- monitor effectiveness
- address your minimum factors
- multiply your church

Building spiritual momentum may seem a bit of a tall order to start with. 'If I could build spiritual momentum I would not need a programme like this!' may well be the response. At its most basic this is largely about longing to see something happen, and thinking carefully what we want as a church. In the last resort, so long as a church is willing to undertake the next step, spiritual momentum should begin to grow. The bottom line should be at the very least some degree of willingness to contemplate change in response to the findings.

The next step is where the NCD process really comes into play. The minister and thirty key members of the church fill in a questionnaire which records their thoughts about the church and about their own spiritual life. The results are fed into a computer analysis program which allows the relative strength of each of the quality characteristics to be evaluated.

To carry this out there are a range of options, from allowing the British Church Growth Association to perform the analysis and write a report to purchasing the computer software and running the analysis yourself. The strength of the questionnaire is that it is aiming to be objective, rather than recording unsupported opinions or prejudices. The questions, mainly statements answered on an agree / disagree scale, do not always give a clear indication of what the 'right' answer might be. The process can only work with the CORE computer program. The results, once received, provide a Church Profile which gives an indication of both the strengths of the church and the minimum factor which is most in need of being addressed.

What is produced is a series of scores, based on the average of national surveys undertaken. The average for each characteristic is 50, with scores below 35 being significantly below average and score above 65 being significantly above average. The key thing, however, is not the overall average of all the characteristics but the lowest single score, since it is this which indicates the all-important minimum factor.

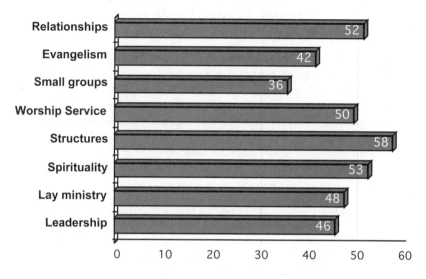

The profile of a sample church

The *Implementation Manual* then guides the church through the steps to be followed in response to the church profile. The emphasis is on:

a) Setting goals which are qualitative rather than quantitative, but which are nevertheless measurable and specific. For example, 'by the end of next year we will have appointed leaders and deputies to oversee each of the main areas of church life,' or (to quote a challenging example from the *Implementation Manual* 'to have ten percent of the participants of the evangelism teaching day discover the gift of evangelism by the end of the year, and to have a personal session with each participant about how he or she can use his or her gifts more effectively towards fulfilling the Great Commission'[6]).
b) Monitoring the effectiveness of the steps taken.
c) Using the strengths to help in addressing the weaker areas.

A further survey six to twelve months later allows evaluation of the progress in church life and establishes the next minimum factor to be tackled. So the process goes on, hopefully producing an ever-healthier church.

6   Schwarz, *Implementation Manual*, p 29.

4

Working with Natural Church Development:
Three Church Stories

How does it work out in practice? What follows are the experiences of churches in three different situations, two of them Anglican and one a local ecumenical partnership. In the first case-study, Paul Reily tells in some detail his own story as the leader of a very ordinary local church working with NCD. From the experience of St Michael's, Westcliff on Sea, we look rather more closely at the figures: just how does a church profile look in practice? Finally, Bar Hill provides a brief case study of a possibility of having your cake and eating it. It is a church which has tried to draw on the principles of NCD without buying into the whole package either literally or metaphorically!

Natural Church Development at St Cedd's Church, Barkingside: One Church Tells Its Story

1. The Background Context of St Cedd's Church, Barkingside

St Cedd's Church, Barkingside, is an urban parish in the London Borough of Redbridge, part of the Diocese of Chelmsford. It has a population of 9,000 of mixed race, culture and religion. The area is predominantly owner occupied, with many 'self-made' entrepreneurs. The only place where you will see more black London taxis than in the parish is Trafalgar Square! Although the church is sixty years old, it almost closed 20 years ago, so it has the feel of a 'young' church, where change comes quite easily. Many of the indigenous Anglican population left then, and have not returned as they settled into neighbouring parish churches. Nobody has a grandfather who installed a stained glass window—there is no stained glass, and very few families can point to more than one generation in the church. The church building is a dual purpose hall.

The church tradition is 'middle of the road,' with an evangelical approach to many things. But church tradition is not the main preoccupation of the congregation.

There has been moderate numerical and spiritual growth over the past 3 years, with a significant emphasis on children's and youth work.

2. How We Got Involved with NCD and Undertook the Survey

I read Christian Schwarz's Natural Church Development (NCD) a couple of years ago and sensed a resonance with his research about church growth. I, like many, have long thought that God is greater than any particular model or approach to church growth. For many the phrase 'church growth' is linked to the guilt of programme following programme, often with few of the promised results being realized. God in his grace would surely be acting out of character if growth depended upon the number of prayer hours we had ratcheted up, or upon the slavish following of some blueprint used by people from an entirely different social, cultural or parochial setting. Here was an approach, not a model, which realistically engaged with some of my concerns about 'growth fixes.'

Thus, after explanation and discussion, and with no small amount of interest, the PCC decided to follow through the process of undertaking a Natural Church Development Survey.

The need to give out 30 questionnaires to the committed and involved membership of the church was easier than it might have been. We were fortunate in that we had 30 people we could give them out to. This is less easy in a small church with fewer people to choose from, which can lead to a false picture of the church since each questionnaire carries more 'weight,' and the more extreme views can be recorded as being more significant than they really are.

The congregation at St Cedd's is a warm and accepting group, and so after explanation people were happy to complete the forms—and it did not cost the PCC many bottles of wine either!

The questionnaires themselves were a challenge to complete. We are not as 'non-book' as some, but all the same the multiple-choice paper presented challenges to many. In part, this was due to the natural apprehension about filling out any form. But in addition, some of the phrases and expressions were difficult even for the theologically trained to understand accurately. One of the greatest difficulties occurred where people just did not understand the concepts. It is true that the process anticipates the questionnaires to be completed by the most committed people in the congregation, but even so, some of our people experienced difficulties with some of the ideas.

The results were analysed by sending the completed questionnaires off to BCGA. There are now a greater number of options for this analysis (including the provision of appropriate software) but it was good to get a personal response and comment on the results, even though this meant that the process took longer.

It would be unfair to say that the whole congregation was collectively holding their breath awaiting the outcome, but there was a ready interest among many to see what we might learn.

When the results came back, we had a more extensive teaching programme about NCD in the Sunday worship and explained the findings to the whole of the congregation.

3. The Results and Where This Took Us

An important aspect of NCD is that it does not claim to be a 'medicine' to solve a church's problems. Rather, it is a diagnostic tool to help in the process of vision setting within the parish context. The local church needs to have a realizable and achievable goal that will enable it to implement its vision. Many of us will have learnt the hard way in ministry where this has not been the case. The analogy of headless chickens comes to mind, as clergy and laity are involved in so many projects and tasks that none are completed satisfactorily.

It is in this context that NCD has one of its greatest uses. It acts to help in the process of discerning where the maximum effort should be placed. We could put effort into all the areas of church life covered by the eight quality characteristics, but we know that that is neither possible nor realistic. By contrast, as a Christian minister, especially working within a broader ministry team, many would feel that they know what the 'Spirit is saying to the church.' But there is no hardship in using a tool to confirm and help in this vision setting, certainly where that tool does not claim to be prescriptive or predictive. There is benefit in the pooling of the wisdom and experience of an approach that has been developed after re-search in over a thousand different churches across the globe to help set our vi-sion.

It is interesting to note that the weakest quality characteristic for St Cedd's was Holistic Small Groups, which was the area that we sensed was our weakest at the start of the process.

With this information gathered, we then set about working on small groups. It is noteworthy that many of the members of these groups have been new people in the life of the church. Indeed, one of the groups is the continuation of a Confir-mation Preparation Group. It is interesting too, that these people represent a sig-nificant part of the spiritual growth within the church. As we reflect upon the people that have come into the life of the church temporarily, and not stayed, we can imagine what might have happened if we had been able to encourage them into the small groups.

Another of the strengths of NCD is the understanding that different areas of church life do not operate in isolation. We have seen this clearly as we observe that with the development of small groups there needs to be a compensating development of lay leadership. This historically has not been an area of great strength at St Cedd's, and consequently we have worked to develop Gift-Orien-tated Lay Ministry as another aim. Again it is interesting to note that this quality characteristic was the second lowest score after Holistic Small Groups. We have sought to do this in part through the development of a broader basis to our wor-ship planning and leadership through the formation of a 'worship team.'

4. The Situation 15 Months Down the Road

We have two small groups that have been running for over a year now and a worship team that is beginning to share in the development of the worshipping life of the church. Whilst we are not seeing great numerical growth in the church, we sense that this has been a good means of consolidating what has gone before, both in recent history with people just confirmed, and with people who have been church members for much of their lives. For many of the latter the small groups have been the first time that they have engaged with their faith in such an immediate way. Admittedly this would not be true for many churches, where such home groups have a long history, but this serves to demonstrate the flexibil-ity of NCD which means that every type of church can benefit from the analysis.

The recommendation from Christian Schwarz is that a subsequent survey is undertaken 6 months following action taken after the first. We have not yet got to this, and many in the BCGA would reckon that a period longer than six months is used, perhaps a year. We are now due to undertake this analysis, and it will be interesting to reflect on the results that are received.

5. Key Learning Points from the Experience

One of the main points that I reflect upon is that St Cedd's was quite a small 'fish' in the deanery. It is not a 'spectacular' church with a huge congregation. In many respects we are where many parishes find themselves—working hard, but not quite getting where we want to be. The vision for the church extends further than just the initiatives that have arisen from NCD. Youth and children's work is a priority, and such areas of ministry as these do not specifically come from one of the eight quality characteristics. That having been said, the use of an approach to church growth that has a high degree of integrity and 'common sense' about it has been a breath of fresh air.

One intuitively knows that the replication of 'successful' approaches elsewhere is not the way forward, and here is an understanding of church growth that engages with this in a realistic way. This is not to decry the success of others, but rather to be realistic about the diversity of parish life, something that not everyone is prepared to take on board!

The 'all by itself' principle which undergirds the NCD approach is also liberating. There has to be more to church growth than hard work. Indeed, we know that so often the harder we work the more we get in God's way. Of course we need to participate with God, but there is a world of difference between participators with God and those who try to do God's work for him. Only God can make the seed grow; it is a growth 'automatism' (catchy little word of Christian Schwarz's) and nothing that we can do can make it grow.[7] But we can provide the right circumstances for it to grow in.

The breadth of spirituality within the Church of England is something that we all celebrate and recognize. One of the real benefits of NCD is that it is not locked into one particular expression of spirituality. Having travelled from the Pentecostal Church to the Church of England, I imagine that I am more 'catholic' than many. I do not rest easy with people who say that a particular spirituality is the only way to know God's blessings of growth. It tends to reveal a very limited understanding of who God is. He is beyond all our imaginings, and boxes too!

The NCD approach is based upon empirical research. It is not a deterministic model that predicts from a point of assertion, but rather guides based upon a huge range of Christian experience taken from every type of church, in every continent and nation. There is an integrity in this that seems to go beyond the political manoeuvring that is associated with some who are devotees of particular models.

---

7   Schwarz, *Natural Church Development*, p 13.

Conclusion

As I am about to move to a new parish, I take with me the experience of how NCD has been applied in the context of St Cedd's. The same principles of vision setting will need to be applied in the new situation, and the important ideas of principles over prescriptive models I am sure will be universally applied. It is not the only tool available, but certainly one that can be useful in the new context.

St Michael's Westcliff on Sea: Looking More Closely at the Profile

St Michael's is a medium-sized parish church in an area of mixed housing on the fringes of Southend with an average Sunday attendance in the region of 160 adults. Peter Nicholson, vicar of St Michael's , discovered Natural Church Development when Schwarz's book was recommended to him. The immediate attractions were the international nature of the research and the 'principles not models' concept underlying the thinking. This seemed a useful tool for producing an effective church audit.

A first set of surveys was distributed among those in positions of lay leadership the the summer of 1997—40 copies to ensure at least 30 were returned. All the PCC were given surveys, plus other lay leaders. The resulting profile emerged:

Empowering Leadership	54	Inspiring worship services	28
Gift-orientated lay ministry	38	Holistic small groups	56
Passionate spirituality	51	Need-orientated evangelism	60
Functional structures	45	Loving relationships	47

St Michael's was committed to on-going evangelism with Peter being a local Alpha resources advisor, so the highest score for evangelism was not an enormous surprise. The low score under inspiring worship services was less expected. St Michael's has a mixed congregation with traditional, charismatic and evangelical strands. Within this mix it may not have been easy to perceive a general dissatisfaction with the quality of worship in the church. On reflection it was agreed that worship had indeed been rather overlooked, and a small NCD team was set up to ensure implementation and to keep goals in sight but realistic. Goals were announced at the Annual Parochial Church Meeting to make the whole congregation aware of the process.

To address worship, the minimum factor, in the first survey, a number of strategies were adopted, partly in response to the guidance in the *Implementation Manual.* Prayer before services, a Saturday workshop on worship, assigning welcomers to each service, a rota for intercessions, job specifications for those involved in worship leading, lay leaders going away on worship conferences—a range of approaches, with the NCD team setting two or three achievable goals at any given time. A new amplification system was put into the church building and new overhead projector.

A second survey eighteen months later revealed not only an improvement in the score relating to worship but also a significant increase in the overall average:

Empowering Leadership	59 (+5)	Inspiring worship services	53 (+25)
Gift-orientated lay ministry	50 (+12)	Holistic small groups	56 (=)
Passionate spirituality	63 (+12)	Need-orientated evangelism	69 (+9)
Functional structures	58 (+13)	Loving relationships	69 (+22)

It would appear from the results of this second survey that the steps adopted to improve the worship at St Michael's were beginning to have a marked effect, but also that something else was going on. The fresh sense of purpose and working together seems to have had the most marked spin-off in encouraging loving relationships, perhaps because a sense of partnership and its practical expression in hospitality will develop as church members set about projects together. Similarly, gifts are put to use, people are more committed in their personal spiritual life since shared action stretches faith and encourages prayer, and structures have to become more functional if things are going to get done by a wide range of church members!

The second survey led to a teaching and action programme on spiritual gifts, while at the same time work continues on developing a vision for worship within the church. A third survey revealed a very marginally lower overall average score, but more significantly a change in the minimum factors with functional structures and holistic small groups (rather left on the back burner, as Peter puts it) now scoring lowest. It was unclear at this stage whether the slightly lower scores represent a neglect of these areas in the light of efforts put into worship and spiritual gifts, or whether rising expectation had produced rather higher expectations on the part of those completing the questionnaires. Certainly the overall rise between the first and second surveys was not repeated, but nor has the progress been lost. The effect on overall church health of a sense that something positive is going on, while not producing ever-rising scores, does seem to result in a lasting and all-round perception that this is a better church to be part of, quite apart from the specific strategies adopted to address the minimum factors.

Following a pattern of gentle decline in the years before NCD was introduced, St Michael's now shows small signs of numerical growth. While not of a scale to be statistically significant, this combines with the growing sense of commitment and expectancy revealed by the surveys to show an overall effect which is extremely positive.

But each church has its own story which will include much beyond those things represent by the NCD surveys. Peter is a strategic thinker, ready both to identify and to use the different resources available and to outline his own approach to those matters which do not seem to have an easily-adopted package available on the Christian scene. Once involved with NCD, he has gone for it wholeheartedly and attended two BCGA courses on using NCD. Good leaders are more likely to have healthy, growing churches whatever the system or approach they use. Other personnel changes have taken place among the lay leadership, and while not part of a formal strategy in response to the NCD surveys, this may have had an important effect in enabling more effective ministry.

St Michael's has been working through a £300,000 building project during the period of the NCD process.While sapping energy and making demands on leadership time, such an undertaking has its own effect in galvanizing God's people, encouraging spiritual commitment (there is nothing like a big projected budget deficit to get us praying!) and releasing gifts which might otherwise lie dormant.

Bar Hill Ecumenical Church: Going Freelance?

How can the NCD approach be used if you do not go the whole hog and use the surveys? Bar Hill is home to a church which has taken on the inspiration of NCD but gone freelance in its implementation.

Bar Hill Church is a busy and thriving ecumenical fellowship at the centre of a new village developed on the edge of Cambridge. Discovering the *Natural Church Development Handbook* in 1997, minister Gary Renison set aside mid-week evening meetings through the autumn of the following year for teaching and discussion on the eight quality characteristics. Every church member who was normally part of a small group joined for this introduction. At the end of the process the whole group completed a home-grown questionnaire asking simply for their opinion of how well the church was meeting each of the quality characteristics.

As a result, gift-oriented ministry was perceived to be the minimum factor. Following a presentation to the annual church meeting in 1999, the eldership undertook a gift audit of all church members, including children. Each was asked to identify his or her own gifts, with the opportunity to talk through the questions with a church elder. In the light of this, a Jubilee process of letting go of things for which people did not feel gifted and a re-offering for ministry in the light of gifting led to a significant reorientation in the staffing and nature of church activities. There was a sense that God had provided all the gifts needed for what the church was called to do, and that it was all right to stop doing some things for which there were not clearly identifiable gifts.

Currently at Bar Hill the focus on gifts continues. The gift audit is set to be repeated, with the Emmaus course used as a means of Christian nurture.

So how effective has the informal approach to NCD proved to be? Certainly the feeling is that it was extremely useful. As with churches which have bought into the full NCD survey approach, addressing one minimum factor had a positive spin-off in other areas of church life. The sense that something positive is going on encourages more in the body of Christ than just one minimum factor-related area. Producing talks to introduce the NCD vision for church health took up considerable time on the part of the minister, although that was certainly seen as time well spent. The quality characteristics were seen as providing full coverage of the essential areas of church life. Of course, the informal approach adopted begs the question of whether formal use of NCD surveys would have produced the same results. There seems to have been general agreement that the minimum factor identified was the right one for understanding church growth in Bar Hill, but the experience of other churches would seem to indicate that sometimes both congregations and church leaders can be surprised by what the surveys produce.

Was Bar Hill's process open to the unexpected in quite the same way?

So far there are no plans to repeat the process from the start. Moving to a gift-oriented approach is seen as a serious, long-term goal with implications for all ages in the life of the church, and it is expected that thorough change in this direction will take up much of the energy of the church for some time. This, together with major building plans, leaves NCD as a significant and highly valued stage in the recent past of Bar Hill Church, but not currently as an important part of the vision for the future. Nevertheless, NCD has played its part as one tool among many as a thoughtfully-led church struggles to work out the appropriate way forward in their specific local situation.

5
So Just How Good Is It? –
Some Questions and Qualifications

The experience of those churches using NCD which have contributed to this study is broadly very positive. Working with Natural Church Development has allowed new insights, sharpened vision, and encouraged focused and appropriate steps towards the future. However, questions remain which, while by no means devaluing the approach, may need consideration if it is to be used to full effect in the contemporary UK context. NCD has also received a perceptive critique from Robert Warren of Springboard,[8] and the evaluation below reflects some of his thinking as well as my own.

NCD Seems to Assume a Relatively Conservative Model of Church Life

The minister (usually assumed to be male) is implied throughout the questionnaires as a single, permanent leadership presence. Although the accompanying notes provide guidance as to how to complete the forms in the absence of one overall leader, the thought world is still largely one in which a single man oversees a single congregation. The quality characteristics, Schwarz's concentration of the qualifying adjectives notwithstanding, assume the existence of certain things (small groups, for example). This may be simple realism in recognizing the most frequent patterns of church life. On the other hand it does not make it easy for a church to broaden its mind about other, more radical patterns of church life—for example, multiple congregations, cells or mid-week worship. The biotic principle of variety within the church makes it unlikely that a series of NCD surveys would

------

8   Robert Warren, 'Healthy Churches' in *Good News* (Board of Mission, Spring 2000).

lead to the establishment of age-specific congregations—although many might see this as a welcome retreat from the homogeneous unit principle which has often been the major stumbling-block in accepting church growth philosophy.

Overall, this may not present insurmountable problems within the Church of England. Female leaders are well used to inclusivizing language, frustrating though that may be, and those involved in experimental forms of church life are probably thoroughly experienced at adaptation. After all, coping with a relatively conservative model is the bread and butter of most Anglican life! However, NCD by itself may not contain much impetus towards radical changes of direction in church structures from inherited to emerging mode (to use Warren's terminology). Radical thinking will have to come from elsewhere, and the NCD categories may need some skilful redefinition.

Working With Natural Church Development Will Be Easier for Some Personality Types Than for Others

Working with NCD, one soon comes across the terminology of plans, goals and programmes. For many people this will be entirely natural, a straightforward expression of thoughtful Christian leadership. For others, there may be a sense of being squeezed into a mould. Some church leaders instinctively delegate tasks to people which are in tune with their spiritual gifts. Some groups and activities 'just happen' in certain churches, especially those which are closely in tune with the normal patterns of life of their local community. Hopefully the wise church leader will recognize that the terminology is simply a way of identifying what he/she/they are already doing, but there may be some good leaders and thoroughly healthy churches who might be put off the approach purely because of questions of language and style.

Can It Work in a UPA Setting?

There are issues to do with language, style, and cost which may make this more challenging than might be the case in suburbia. People in most churches might look puzzled, to say the least, when hit with the terminology of 'biotic principles' or the dangers of the 'super-spiritual paradigm.' The difference is probably that educated suburbanites might feel more obliged to look like they understand it. In a UPA setting the responsibility of the leader to translate will be even more important. Even terms like 'passionate spirituality' might need translation into something like 'getting really excited about knowing God.' I suspect that some work on translation would be very healthy in most settings, and might provide a good check on how well things are being understood.

One church leader has reported the confusion of people in a non-book culture when faced with job descriptions. Certainly the NCD package has the feel of being most suited to people who are comfortable with the language of goals, roles and strategies. Again, this places more responsibility on the shoulders of the leader to become an adaptor and translator, and makes it even less easy to use NCD undigested.

The question of cost is perhaps less significant. The total budget needed to work with NCD is dwarfed by most organ funds. For many churches this is simply a question of priorities. For those where the expenditure is genuinely more than can be managed it may perhaps be a challenge to deanery, diocese or surrounding parishes about their priorities and the need for Anglicans to remember that they are not at root congregationalists but have a responsibility for the life and health of other local churches around them.

Is It Fundamentally About Natural Congregational Development?

Although develop by a German Lutheran, NCD seems remarkably focused on the congregation as the fundamental expression of church. There is little relevance to church life at a wider scale, for example the diocese. The sections in the *Implementation Manual* which look at spiritual gifts appear to assume that they will be overwhelmingly employed within the life of the congregation rather than the wider community. Question 43 in the congregational questionnaire asks for relative agreement or disagreement with the statement: 'My faith is transforming the way that I live (*eg* profession, family, spare time etc),' but this does not appear to be followed up in the proposals on spiritual gifts in the *Implementation Manual*. Indeed, the use of key lay leaders to provide the thirty congregation surveys may skew the results towards the experiences and perceptions of those most involved in the life of the congregation and less involved in outside activities.

> All your workers who fill out a questionnaire should have, if possible, the following characteristics:
> a) The minister considers them to be actively involved *at the very centre of church life.*
> b) They should have a *regular task* in the church.
> c) They should be a member of a small group in the church (a cell group, Bible study group, ministry team etc) and cover a wide variety of active church members.[9]

Many churches may quite rightly believe it is their goal to grow as a congregation, and healthier congregations should be good news for the wider community and for the wider church, but it is important that churches setting out to use NCD materials are aware of this starting point.

Maybe it is helpful to develop the analogy of the healthy body here. Body-building for its own sake has a very limited value, but a fit body put to work in the service of others is of far greater value.

Schwarz's biotic imagery could be easily and effectively extended to encourage a whole-life orientation of Christian discipleship.

---

9   Schwarz, *Implementation Manual*, p 12 (Italics original).

What About Justice and Peace Issues?

Should a healthy church be fighting for justice and peace in the world? This is not a question asked within the NCD survey process, and it is possible to score highly with regard to the eight quality characteristics without even considering injustice in the world around. Schwarz in *Paradigm Shift* provides a rationale for this (pp 189–199). Perhaps reflecting his Lutheran background he sees campaigning on wider issues as a parachurch responsibility whereas the local church is expected to focus on needs-orientated evangelism. Robert Warren has questioned this, since needs-orientated evangelism lays itself open to the danger of creating dependent client groups.[10]

More significant, perhaps, is the danger that focusing on felt needs may be effective evangelistically but does little to address blatant injustices which may go unrecognized by the local population. Thus racism may be a keenly felt problem in some urban areas, but may not be thought to be an issue in an all-white rural setting where racist attitudes may actually be deeply entrenched. The problems of disenchanted young people who hang around the streets in a visible way may be much more of a felt need than equally needy lonely old people who experience invisible suffering behind closed doors. Not all needs are felt by everyone!

An Overwhelmingly Adult Concept of the Church is Assumed

This is, I believe, potentially the greatest weakness in NCD as it currently exists. In the light of Peter Brierly's deeply alarming observations of the disappearance of much Christian children's and youth work,[11] it is disappointing that the only question in the congregational questionnaire which addresses children and young people asks for relative agreement with the statement that children are 'well cared-for during services' (Q62). If there is to be hope for the church in future generations, churches using NCD analysis have a responsibility to maintain a commitment to excellent children's and young people's work as a top priority. There is a limit to how long any congregation can stay healthy, if its average age is steadily rising. This is a major area for concern, and needs to be consciously addressed by any church using NCD.

The Diagnostic Value of NCD Is Not (At Least Not Yet) Matched by Similar Ease of Use as a Tool for Transformation

As the experience of some of the churches above has shown, the analysis of church health provided by a NCD survey can be extremely revealing. It is, however, one thing to know what is wrong and another to be able to change it. In some cases the very indication of an area of weakness will allow prayer and energy to be directed towards it, and the church may have easy access to ideas and resources which can help. In other cases, awareness of a weakness which was already suspected without accompanying tools to make the necessary changes

---

10   Warren, 'Healthy Churches.'
11   Peter Brierly, *The Tide is Running Out* (Christian Research, 2000) chap 4.

may increase frustration.

One possible cause of this frustration may be the tendency of churches and church leaders to run out of steam in working though the NCD materials. The eight quality characteristics and the minimum-factor barrel are easily grasped and easily communicated, and the impact of this alone should not be underestimated. It is less straightforward to assimilate and explain such principles as 'energy transformation' or 'multiple-usage'—not only because they come later in the books and may be encountered when the average hard-pressed church leader is already flagging somewhat! The 'biotic' approach contains considerable wisdom, but suffers from a lack of translated materials so that the injunction to 'use biotic tools' may be more easily said than done. The Natural Church Development book has an encouraging display of training materials pictured in full colour, but unfortunately on inspection the reader will see that all the titles are in German. Those sections of training material I have encountered prior to publication in the UK have looked extremely promising, and teaching material on Gift-Oriented Ministry is next in line for translation,[12] but it will be some time before all the training material is available in translation.

Christian Schwarz seems aware of the potential pitfalls in this area, and in a helpful section in the *Implementation Manual* (p 196) identifies as the most frequent mistake of churches using the NCD approach that of discovering the minimum factor in church life but only talking about rather than addressing the issues. Similarly, the danger of carrying out only one survey and failing to follow it up with another to monitor progress is mentioned on more than one occasion.

There is, of course, a wealth of material in English on church growth which is not available in the German-speaking world, but this is not always directly applicable to the specific quality characteristics identified by NCD. There will be more work involved for the local church in locating, adapting and using materials from other sources as they try to respond to the relative weaknesses of the minimum factor revealed by the NCD survey. One church leader has commented that this is potentially an advantage, since it opens up the possibility of a great degree of flexibility.

At present, however, the responsibility for finding materials lies largely with the local church. The availability in translation of more NCD material may make for easier implementation, but may also lead to NCD becoming more of an all-encompassing package with less local autonomy in the way it is adopted.

A New Paradigm—Or a Useful Tool for the Box?

Given the reservations and questions just expressed, just how valuable is Natural Church Development? The claim that this is a new paradigm for the church is perhaps a little over-ambitious. Contemporary British culture is not a

---

12 For current details, contact British Church Growth Association, The Park, Moggerhanger, Bedford, MK44 3RW, info@bcga.org.uk, http://www.bcga.org.uk. The BCGA also have some recent comment on NCD which begins to address some of the questions raised here.

comfortable cradle for sustained church growth. Were there an easily used panacea available it would have been discovered long ago and church attendance figures would be revealing significant results. Schwarz's work is rather part of a shift in church growth thinking away from numbers and towards church health. As one of the main agents for change in this direction it is of immense value, and worthy of far more attention and of far wider usage than has been the case to date in the UK. In many ways it has the feel of church growth thinking without the bits which many people for many years have instinctively felt to be less acceptable.

In reminding us of the promise of Jesus, 'I will build my church,' Natural Church Development takes some of the weight of guilt and anxiety off congregations and church leaders. There is a liberating feeling about forgetting numerical targets and focusing on the quality of church life. In celebrating diversity, recognizing different gifts and encouraging mutual support, NCD has the potential to allow each church to grow in its own way, with a mixture of types and groups of people involved together.

In adopting NCD the local church is setting out with a programme which aims to allow focused effort in the directions most appropriate for the specific situation. But the challenge to the leadership of the local church is still to be not merely adopters but adapters. Wise use of NCD, as with any other programme, will involve thinking through its recommendations in the light of the local context and pondering how the results stack up against the leaders' own awareness of the practical and spiritual issues surrounding them. Tools are made to be used, not swallowed, and while a good tool, NCD still needs to be used wisely, critically, and with the recognition that it is just one tool in the box we have at our disposal.

There are questions to be asked of NCD, but these in no way outweigh the importance of what I believe to be work of very great significance for the future of the church in the contemporary world. If we believe that the natural growth of the church is indeed part of God's plan for creation, then the NCD programme deserves at least serious consideration from every congregation. To quote Paul Reily from St Cedd's, Barkingside:

> Whilst we have the responsibility to be co-workers with God, and to remove the hindrances to growth, we are not responsible for that growth. I cannot make a seed grow, although I can plant it and water it and give it the right conditions for growth. It grows by itself, because of what God has placed within it. This is more in line with a biblical understanding of the Creator God, from whom all good things flow.